Jesus Said Unto Her,

"Talitha Cumi"

*And commanded that something should
be given her to eat (Mark 5:43)*

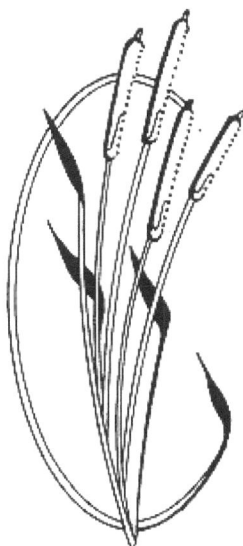

Jesus Said Unto Her,

"Talitha Cumi"

And commanded that something should be given her to eat (Mark 5:43)

by

Dr. Juanita Crawford

Ed. D, MSN, RN

Senior Publisher
Steven Hill

ASA Publishing Corporation

ASA Publishing Corporation

An Accredited Publishing House with the BBB

105 E. Front St., Suite 101

Monroe, Michigan 48161

www.asapublishingcorporation.com

Copyrights©2017 Juanita Crawford, All Rights Reserved

Title: Jesus Said Unto Her, "Talitha Cumi"

Date Published: 01.16.2017 / Edition 1 *Trade Paperback*

Book ID: ASAPCID2380718

ISBN: 978-0-9977790-6-6

Library of Congress Cataloging-in-Publication Data

This book was published in the United States of America.

State of Michigan

FOREWORD

WHAT IS SO SPECIAL ABOUT A CHILD'S HEART? WHY ARE CHILDREN SPECIAL IN GOD'S SIGHT? THE ANSWERS: CHILDREN ARE SPECIAL TO GOD, EVEN BEFORE THEY ARE BORN AND GOD KNOWS AND REMEMBERS THEM ALL (ISAIAH 49:15; JEREMIAH 1:5) ON A PERSONAL BASIS. THEY ARE A HERITAGE OF GOD AND A BLESSING FROM GOD TO THEIR PARENTS (PSALM 127 3-4). GOD IS GREATLY PLEASED WITH INDIVIDUALS WHO ARE HUMBLE AND HAVE CHILDISH CHARACTERISTICS. CHILDREN ARE NOT TO BE OVERLOOKED, FOR THE KINGDOM OF HEAVEN BELONGS TO THEM (MATTHEW 19: 14-15). WE AS ADULTS ARE TO LEAD OUR CHILDREN TO GOD IN A MANNER WHICH IS UNDERSTANDABLE TO THEM, AND ENCOURAGE THEM IN ALL THAT THEY DO. I AM HUMBLED AND PRIVILEGED TO WRITE A FICTIONAL BOOK ON THE BEHALF OF MY LITTLE CHRISTIAN SISTER PIER, AND MY PRAYER IS THAT SHE AND EACH READER ARE EDIFIED AND ENLIGHTENED.

DEDICATION

(*Above* - Pier with her Uncle and Aunt)

This book is dedicated to Pier Chrystal Fisher a 13 year old Christian friend of mine who approached me on June 21, 2015 (*with a Child's Heart*) and asked me, *why don't you write a children's book*? I had the privilege of teaching her while substituting in the children's Sunday School Class. Pier attends church with her Uncle: Deacon Arthur Allen Walker, and Aunt: Sis. Gloria Dean Walker (also her guardians). Pier is a member of the Usher board, Sunday school, and has been taking piano lessons since the age of nine. In my humble opinion, she is progressing beautifully. Little Ms. Fisher's goals and desires are to become a great pianist, to play for her church, and to become a physician. She is always gracious and states, *thank you Sister Crawford for being one of my Sunday school teachers.* While this is not a children's book, it is a book for youths (Godspeed Pier, and Thank you). This book is also dedicated to my grandchildren, great grandchildren, nieces, nephews, and all the youths of the world. May God's everlasting Grace and Mercy continue to embrace you all, Agape!

ACKNOWLEDGEMENTS

I give reverence to my Lord and Savior Jesus Christ for allowing me to write my 3rd book. *Heavenly Father, I thank you for granting me patience and endurance to continue to write (fiction and non-fiction) materials to your Glory and all readers' edification.* To my husband (Rev. Emmett Crawford Jr.), thank you for the initial phase of proof-reading and editing this book.

All Scriptures quoted and paraphrased are taken from the Holy Bible (KJV), unless otherwise denoted

Table of Contents

Jesus Said Unto Her,

"Talitha Cumi"

*And commanded that something should
be given her to eat (Mark 5:43)*

by

Dr. Juanita Crawford

Ed. D, MSN, RN

CHAPTER 1
INTRODUCTION

𝕮hildren are very important to parents, grandparents, siblings, other children, the survival of society, and most importantly Jesus. In fact, it is with a child's heart that one must enter into heaven. In Matthew 18: 1-4, when the disciples asked Jesus who is the greatest in the kingdom of heaven, Jesus "called a little child unto him, and set him in the midst of them, and said, verily I say unto you, except ye be converted (changed), and become as little children, ye shall not enter into the kingdom of heaven." Jesus went on to say, "Whosoever therefore shall humble (become lowly) himself as this little child, the same is greatest in the kingdom of heaven. And whoso shall receive one such little child in my name receiveth me. But whoso shall offend (upset) one of these little ones which believe in me, it were better for him that a **millstone** were hanged about his neck, and that he were drowned in the depth (deepness) of the sea (Matthew 18: 4-6).

𝔜es, children are very important to God and their personalities are key features in becoming a part of the kingdom of God. Children tend to have a *pure heart* and want to help others. A study found that toddlers (before potty trained) are regularly motivated by compassion when helping others rather than receiving praise for doing good deeds, this may be related to an inwardly deep-rooted concern for others (Kennedy, 2012). Max Plank Institute for Evolutionary Anthropology researchers conducted a study on 56 *two year olds*, divided them into groups of three's and let them observe an adult dropping a crayon or a can. All groups struggled to pick the items up (Kennedy, 2012).

Even more touching, recently in Wyandotte, Michigan, some neighborhood children gave a carwash (also solicited on Facebook) to raise money for a homeless man to buy him something to eat. The children raised $500 to assist this stranger and their mothers set out to seek this homeless man shelter. One of the children made the stranger a sandwich, gave him a fruit cup and a yogurt. Touched by this compassion, the homeless man started to cry. The stranger informed the children that he had recently suffered a heart attack and after returning home found his home destroyed by fire (Hudson, 2016). *Lord, bless these children!*

Children have important commonalities that are pleasing to God. Strehler (2016), find that children are sinners by nature, but want to be good. They love stories and have loaded imaginations. Children prefer victory over evil, like singing, performing, and being imaginative. They are very expressive, aware, cheery, helpless, forgiving, and forget with no trouble. Children are easily discouraged, good at memorizing, eager to learn, anxious to gain skills, are trusting, and believe what adults tell them. Strehler (2016) goes on to describe the uniqueness of children *raised up in God fearing homes* and find that these children are more likely to believe in God, trust Jesus as their friend, have no problem with praying, considers God as having the power to answer prayer, and believes all things written in the Bible are true. All parents have the responsibility of raising and training up their children in a God-fearing way (Proverbs 22:6). When parents are not available, other adults (particularly Christians) should assist in guiding, caring, and training up the child/children in a Godly manner. In a world of constant disorder and hacvoc, children need encouragements; they need to know Jesus and His Miraculous Power. So I say to all the children of the world who have great dreams and desires, *"Talitha Cumi."* Trust God, *"Arise, shine; for thy light is come, and the Glory of the LORD is risen upon thee" (Isaiah 60:1).*

While the Miracle of *"Talitha Cumi"* is a true story of a 12 year old girl raised from the dead by Jesus Christ in the Holy Bible (Mark 5:41), this book is fictional and tells of a 10 year old girl name Cindy Tucker who learns to love Jesus and strives to become a singer while struggling with her dysfunctional family and non-supporting peers. The moral of this fictional story in a true sense is for parents (in particular) and everyone else to love, embrace, support, encourage, and uplift our children. In today's society, full of uncertainty and destruction, no one should ever destroy a child's dreams or desires as displayed in this fictional story about Cindy. No one knows the future of our children, and our duty as parents are to encourage and teach them to have faith in God. Only God knows our children's future as He states in His word, "For I know the plans I have for you," declares the LORD, "plans to prosper you and not to harm you, plans to give you hope and a future" (Jeremiah 29:11; NIV).

Cindy, while growing up in her neighborhood (at the age of four) was introduced by her mother to an elderly Christian woman name Ms. Bertha Jones, who befriends and encourages Cindy to hold on to her faith, beliefs, and dreams. Bertha (known as Mother Bertha since she regularly took children under her wing) often told Cindy about Jesus, the story of "*Talitha Cumi*," and how to use this life given miracle to reach her goals.

Talitha Cumi (Mark 5:41) is a Syriac or Aramaic expression meaning little maid arise (Bible Study Tools, 2014). While the disciples: Peter, James, and John (the brother of James) were present with Jesus when He performed this miracle, it was Peter who told of this miracle to John Mark (the author of the book of Mark in the Holy Bible). According to Theopedia (n.d.), John Mark was a Palestinian Jew, the cousin of Barnabas (Colossians 4:10), early traveling companion of Apostle Paul (Acts 12:25), and a spiritual son of Peter (1st Peter 5:13).

The story of Talitha Cumi is found in a combination of miracles of Jesus found in the gospels of Matthew 9:18-26, Mark 5:21-43, and Luke 8:40-56. In paraphrasing the story concerning *Talitha Cumi* (Mark 5: 35-42): a Ruler (by the name of Jarius; Luke 8:41) of the synagogue 12 year old daughter died. Jesus told the ruler to fear not, but only believe. Jesus then instructs no one to follow him except Peter, James, and John (the brother of James) as He goes to the ruler's home. Upon entering the ruler's home Jesus finds many people crying and weeping greatly. Jesus asked them, why such an uproar? He then states, the child is not dead, only asleep. The people begin to laugh and disrespect Jesus; He puts everyone out of the house except Peter, James, John, and the child's parents. Jesus then walks over to the girl (lying in bed), takes her hand, and says to her, "*Talitha Cumi*" and the little girl immediately arose and walked. Now, everyone was greatly amazed. Jesus instructs everyone not to tell of this miracle and to

give the little girl something to eat. *Praise the Lord!*

CHAPTER 2
THE STORY OF CINDY

Cindy 10, was the youngest of three children (sister Rita 15, and brother Ralph 12) born to Mr. Robert and Bernice Tucker, who resided in Grosse Pointe Farms, Michigan. Mr. Tucker was well educated and worked as a Bank Manager. Mrs. Tucker worked as a teacher's aide. The Tuckers purchased their home 14 years ago after Mr. Tucker hit the lottery. They appeared to be a happy go lucky family (rarely went to church) and gave numerous house parties. Cindy's sister and brother for the most part, were always hanging out with their friends and did not want to be bothered with Cindy. Other than visiting Ms. Bertha, one could find Cindy at home reading her Bible, doing homework, and completing her chores. She was known to many as a loner.

Although Cindy was not reared up in church she was very curious about God and was allowed to attend church (started at age four) with Ms. Bertha Jones, who lived several houses down from the Tuckers. Ms. Bertha was wealthy, well known in the neighborhood, and around the world. She was recognized on the block (lived in her mansion for 35 years) as *Mother Bertha* because she often acted as a caregiver for many of her neighbors' children. Mother Bertha was a 70 year old widower, a highly respected Christian (attended church faithfully), and a renown (popular) retired plastic surgeon. Her husband passed away 15 years ago. Everyone seemed to love Mother Bertha, she loved Jesus, and showed love to everyone she met. Regularly, children would come by to visit her, she would read them children Bible stories, teach them about Jesus, and feed them healthy meals and treats.

Often Mother Bertha welcomed them to attend church services with her. Some of the children attended on special days such as Easter and Christmas, but Cindy went as often as her mom would allow. Cindy loved visiting with Mother Bertha, she learned to love Jesus, and really enjoyed going to church. Often she would be

teased by her sister Rita and friends who called her
"*little miss church girl.*"

Cindy would often
cry and tell her parents
about the teasing, but they
would always tell her, "*girl,
just grow up, don't you see
we are busy.*"   Although
Cindy's   brother   Ralph
didn't tease her, he showed no interest in her at all. Of
course he was in his own 12-year old world, running
around with his so called friends who frequently
skipped school and spent most of their time hanging out
on street corners. Cindy's parents were aware of what
Ralph was doing but did nothing, for they were always
busy working and having home parties with their
friends.

Frequently Cindy would run to Mother Bertha
and tell her about the teasing. Mother Bertha was never
too busy for Cindy and took the time to comfort,
encourage, give her a big hug, and tell her that God
loves her and so did she. Mother Bertha would then read
Cindy a Bible story, for Cindy loved Bible stories and
often felt better afterwards; until she
returned home. To overlook the teasing,
Cindy would spend a lot of time in her
room singing, she loved singing and had
been singing since she was 5 years of age.
Yet, no one could stand her singing and
often told her to *please be quiet.* Cindy,
although ignoring their remarks, continued to sing in a
lower tone. Cindy loved singing and personally felt she
was pretty good at it, so she decided to let others hear

(what she called) her glorious voice.

CHAPTER 3
CINDY'S DESIRE

One day while eating dinner at home with her parents and sister (Ralph is not at home), Cindy excitedly informed them that she would like to sing in her school's talent show. Her father said, "*girl, you don't have time for that foolishness.*" Her mother stated, "*no one in their family could sing and neither can you!*" Her sister Rita started laughing and teasing her, this time calling her "*little miss church going want-to-be-singer.*" Cindy was highly disappointed, and asked to be excused. After being excused, she ran to her room and started crying. Cindy couldn't wait to visit with Mother Bertha, for she knew that she would feel better after speaking with her.

Upon returning home from school Cindy asked her mother if she could go and visit Mother Bertha. Her mom being busy talking with one of her lady friends told her it was okay. Cindy still feeling sad and weary called Mother Bertha and asked if she could come over to visit, Mother Bertha stated, "*sure dear!*" Upon arrival, Mother Bertha gave Cindy a big hug and offered her some cake.

Cindy began to tell Mother Bertha what happened when she told her family she would like to sing in the school's talent show. She went on to tell Mother Bertha how much she loves to sing and that one day she will become a great Gospel singer, singing praises to the Lord. Cindy stated, "Mother Bertha, I am very sad right now because my family do not believe in my dreams; they never encourage or support what I want to do." Cindy also told Mother Bertha that one day she will become a great physician just like her. Mother Bertha smiled and stated, "don't' worry Cindy about the comments your family made, and just pray for them. God knows your feelings and desires. God already knew this day would come, for His Word says, "even the youths shall faint and be weary" (Isaiah 40:30)."

"Be encouraged Cindy, God will strengthen, take care of you, and grant you the desires of your heart, if it's His will. I certainly have faith in you" . . . and she smiled. Mother Bertha told Cindy, in order for her to become a physician she must study hard in school, and keep her grades up. "Never give up Cindy, and remember you can do all things through Christ who strengthens you (Philippians 4:13, paraphrased), and as far as the singing, can you sing a little bit for me?"

Cindy jumped up from the table and starting singing a song that she heard the children sing in the youth choir at Mother Bertha's church. The song was . . . *"Yes, Jesus Loves Me, Yes, Jesus Loves Me, Yes . . . Jesus Loves Me . . . for the Bible tells Me So."* Cindy did not know all the words to the song so she made up some. Mother Bertha just smiled. Upon completion of the song, Mother Bertha told her that it was good, but they would work together to improve her singing. For many years Mother Bertha had sang in the adult choir at her church, and was pretty good at it, she also played the piano.

Cindy (appearing saddened) asked Mother Bertha, "What do you suggest I do to better my singing?" Lets me see Mother Bertha stated, "First, let us pray to God about it." "Okay," Cindy said. Mother Bertha and Cindy kneeled down to pray.

Mother Bertha prayed a long and powerful prayer. She began by stating, *"Dear Heavenly, most powerful God; we come to you giving you all the praises and honor you so worthily deserve. We pray that in Jesus' name you hear our prayer."* "Please hear us Lord", Cindy stated. Mother Bertha continued, *"Heavenly Father, your little servant Cindy is troubled right now; please comfort her and forgive those who have saddened her. Please draw them near and dear to you."*

"Father God . . . , please grant Cindy the desires of her heart, if it's your will, for she loves you and chases after your own heart. Bless her with a glorious voice, so that when she sings the angels in heaven and all listeners will be edified. Please Father; bless her above and beyond the means you have granted me, in which I humbly and graciously thank you. For you said in your Word (paraphrasing Deuteronomy 2:1-13) that if we, your servants, would abide in you and keep your commandments that you would elevate us above all

nations and give us overflowing blessings. Father, you said that we would be blessed in the city, in the field, and that the fruit of our body, grounds, and cattle would be blessed.

Merciful God, you said that our storehouses would be filled, and that we will be blessed coming and going. Father, your Words says that you will smite our enemies before our faces, bless our land, make us holy unto thee in that everyone will know that we belongs to you to the point that they will recognize you as Lord, and fear you. Gracious Father, your Word reminds us that you will bless us in a mighty way if we continue to serve you. We believe your Word which states that you will bless our hands in that we will lend and not borrow, be the head and not the tail, and that we will be above and not beneath. We thank you Heavenly Father for these blessings you have spoken over us and we have faith that all things are possible through you. Please Father God, anoint little Cindy's hands in a miraculous way as she plays the piano to your Glory." Mother Bertha ended the prayer by placing her hands on Cindy's throat and stating, *"by the power vested in me by God the Father, Son, and the Holy Ghost, in Jesus Name . . . "Talitha Cumi," Amen."*

What a powerful prayer Mother Bertha prayed on the behalf of Cindy. Mother Bertha spoke of *Talitha Cumi* to encourage, empower, and remind Cindy that through Christ these problems and issues will be resolved, if she only trusts God. The Word of God tells us in Luke 10:19 (paraphrased) that God have given us power to overcome all challenges, even the power of the enemy, and nothing will harm us. After we become Christians' and keep our faith in the Lord, God gives us the power and authority through Jesus Christ to overcome challenges we may encounter (even in havoc times). We must however, speak the resolution in existence.

Cindy knew about the story of Jesus and the little girl He brought back to life after stating "*Talitha Cumi*". In fact, this was one of her favorite Bible stories that Mother Bertha had read to her. She thanked Mother Bertha for praying and believing in her. Mother Bertha begins to practice voice lessons with Cindy . . . going over and over various gospel songs until Cindy became very tired. "Don't worry Cindy", Mother Bertha stated, "we can practice as much as your parents will allow you to come over and visit me, and I will also teach you to play the piano." Cindy was so excited, she never told anyone about her singing or piano lessons with Mother Bertha, and she only sung at home when no one was there. Mother Bertha asked Cindy if she would also like to take piano and voice lessons with one of her friends. "Yes," Cindy stated, "but I am not sure if my parents would allow me to take the lessons." "Don't worry Cindy, I will come over and ask them," Mother Bertha stated. "Thank you so very much Mother Bertha, you are so wonderful," Cindy stated, she smiled and gave Mother Bertha a big hug.

One day after Cindy visited with Mother Bertha, she asked her to come home with her. Mother Bertha loved Cindy and replied "yes." Upon entering Cindy's home, her parents were sitting on the couch (Rita and Ralph were not home) and offered

Mother Bertha a seat. Mother Bertha happily greeted Cindy's parents, thanked them for the seat and then informed Cindy's parents the reason for her short visit. Mother Bertha boldly asked if it would be alright if Cindy took piano lessons at no cost to them. She informed Cindy's parents that the piano lessons will be scheduled for three times a week, after school, and that she will take care of all the expenses.

Mother Bertha purposely did not inform Cindy's parents about the voice lessons included with this package, since her parents did not like her singing. Cindy's parents agreed the lessons were fine, as long as the piano lessons did not interfere with Cindy's schooling and chores. Cindy was greatly appreciative of Mother Bertha, and thanked her. Cindy began to work harder in school, became an honor student, did her chores at home, attended voice and piano lessons faithfully, and continued to visit Mother Bertha almost every day.

Cindy (**now 13 years of age**, Mother Bertha now 73) had been taking voice and piano lessons for three years. During this time she continued to attend church, visit, and now care for Mother Bertha. One day while visiting with Mother Bertha, Cindy was asked to sing a song. Mother Bertha decided to test the waters of *God's Divine power* by hearing Cindy's progress. Cindy was very gracious and excited to sing for Mother Bertha, but this time she went over to Mother Bertha's baby grand piano, sat down, played an intro, and begins to sing. The title of the song was, *"Bow down, if you want the Lord to help you, bow down."* Cindy knew all of the verses and not only sung with a powerful soprano voice, but showed sincere facial emotions. Surprisingly, Cindy stood up from the piano, continued to sing, kneeled down on her knees with out-stretched arms to the heavens, . . . and her soprano voice echoed so high in pitch that the glasses shook in Mother Bertha's china cabinet.

Cindy ended the song by standing up, moving her arms, and walking around making emotional body gestures. It was as if she was performing on stage in front of an audience. When she finished the song Mother Bertha was spiritually edified and so amazed that tears ran down her face, chills ran up her spine, and the hairs on her arms stood up. She grabbed Cindy and stated *"what a beautiful, powerful, inspirational voice you have developed"* (now wiping the tears). "Oh my God, have mercy Lord," she stated.

Mother Bertha asked Cindy, *"Have you sung for your family recently?"* "No," Cindy answered (appearing gloomy), "they do not like it when I sing, and are not interested in my dream of becoming a famous gospel singer. I would love to sing for them and anyone that will listen, I love to sing for the Lord," Cindy stated. Cindy went on to say, "Mother Bertha, my family is not religious and I love God. Every time I try to talk to them about God they tell me to keep the sermon to myself. I have been praying to God to help them to come to Him, but nothing has changed. My parents continue to party, my sister and brother both quit school, and now hangs out all night long with their friends. What am I going to do Mother Bertha?" Cindy pauses and states . . . "If I didn't have you Mother Bertha, I don't know what I would do?"

Mother Bertha took Cindy by the hand and stated, "Cindy have you forgotten what I taught you about Jesus and how He can solve all problems?" "No I haven't forgotten about Jesus Mother Bertha, I just want things to change right now and it hasn't happened, although I pray to God every night. I love my parents, sister, and brother, and I want them to love, accept, and encourage me; just like you do. Although I forgive them for treating me this way, it still hurts Mother Bertha. I wish they would just give me a chance to sing to them." Again mother Bertha hugs Cindy, takes her by the hand and states, "Let us pray Cindy." Together they bow down on their knees and Mother Bertha begins to pray a short prayer, she ends the prayer again with "*Talitha Cumi*" in regards to Cindy's family relationship. Mother Bertha and Cindy now have dinner.

Mother Bertha asked Cindy if she would like to become a member of her church. Cindy, highly excited stated "Yes!" "We must first ask your parents if it's okay for you to join," stated Mother Bertha. "Yes, Mother Bertha, I will ask them tomorrow," Cindy stated. Cindy (overly excited) spent several hours with Ms. Bertha and returned home.

CHAPTER 4
A NEW CHRISTIAN
CONVERT, PRAISE GOD!

Cindy, after returning home from school was very excited and during dinner asked her parents if she could join the church Mother Bertha attended. Mrs. Tucker stated, *"That's fine with me as long as I don't have to buy you any new clothes."* Mr. Tucker agreed on one condition, that being, Cindy slept over with Mother Bertha on Saturdays so he wouldn't be disturbed while she was getting ready for church on Sundays. Although Cindy was pleased with her parent's response to freely join the church, she was disappointed they did not mention coming to see her join. Cindy decided to

ask her parents to be sure. She stated, "Mom . . . Dad .
. ., are you both going to come and see me join the
church?" They both stated, *"No"*, at the same time.

How sad this must have been for Cindy, she left
the dinner table quietly and went to her room in tears.
Cindy was so sad, she begin to kneel on her knees and
pray to God for comfort. She remembered what Mother
Bertha taught her regarding Jesus comforting those that
need to be comfort. Her prayer was: *"Dear God, please
make me stronger and not to hurt so bad when my
parents won't support me. In the name of Jesus, please
help my parents, sister, and brother come to know and
love you like I do. Father, please make me a good
church member and help people to like and not tease
me. Father God, Mother Bertha told me that you can
change people and their hearts and I believe that. Dear
God, thank you for putting Mother Bertha on this earth
to love, care, and teach me about you. Thank you for
allowing her to send me for voice and piano lessons. If
it's your will Father God, bless me with a powerful
voice to sing praises to you, for you are worthy, and I
love you. Please Father God comfort me, for I am
hurting right now and I need you to relive me of this
pain . . . in Jesus Name, "Talitha Cumi" Amen."*

Saturday night Cindy spent the night with
Mother Bertha, went to church and joined. Mother
Bertha was so pleased; she practically adopted Cindy
and often spoiled her by buying her very expensive
dresses and matching shoes. Several weeks later Cindy
joined the youth choir and the director and musician was
so amazed at her voice that they often let her lead songs
and sing solos.

Mother Bertha was so excited she invited some of her influential friends to visit at church with her just to hear Cindy sing. One of Mother Bertha's influential friends (Mr. Gabriel Wright) was a producer and owned a recording studio. After hearing Cindy's voice, he was astounded and wanted to sign her right away with a recording contract.

Cindy and Mother Bertha were very excited but did not know how Cindy's parents would accept this offer. Before approaching Cindy's parents, Mother Bertha hired her personal lawyer friend (Mr. Sam Plenty) to assist her in reading and clearly understanding the contract (even though the producer was her friend). Mother Bertha then explained the contract to Cindy. The contract stated that it would by no means interfere with Cindy's schooling, church services, and that she could

come and record in her spare time. *What a deal!* The producer (highly desperate) wanted Cindy's parents to sign a contract authorizing her to sing for his record company. In his opinion, her voice was unique,

powerful, and inspirational. He voiced, "At such a young age *thirteen* the world would really love to hear this angel sing." Cindy was so happy and sad at the same time because she was thinking . . . what if her parents said no, like they always had in regards to her singing? Cindy became so nervous she asked Mother Bertha to come with her to ask her parents. Mother Bertha said, "Okay Cindy, keep the faith, and let us go."

CHAPTER 5
MOM AND DAD, CAN I SING?

Cindy and Mother Bertha entered Cindy's home to find her parents arguing over unpaid bills. Cindy was so embarrassed; she softly spoke to her parents and told them that Mother Bertha would like to talk with them for minute. "What is it now?" Cindy's mom asked. "Are you in some type of trouble, Cindy's father stated?" Mother Bertha greeted her parents and informed them that Cindy was not in trouble at all. Cindy's parents both sitting on the couch asks Mother Bertha to have a seat. Cindy (looking very nervous) sat next to Mother Bertha who informed her parents (due to their arguing) that she would not keep them long but wanted to know if they would allow Cindy to sing and record some gospel songs. Mother Bertha informs them that they both would have to sign the contract due to Cindy's age.

Mother Bertha went on to say, "I have reviewed the contract with my lawyer Mr. Sam Plenty, who is a dear friend of mine and he approves it. The producer Mr. Gabriel Wright is also a friend of mine and I wouldn't let anything happen to my Cindy, for she is like a daughter to me. Here is the contract for your reviewing, and if you both approve you can both sign it. By no means will this contract interfere with her schooling, chores, or going to church." "Are you serious," stated Mr. Tucker, "with that terrible voice of hers?" He begins to laugh. Mrs. Tucker, on the other hand stated, "I don't care, and signed the contract immediately." She was still upset regarding their argument. Mr. Tucker stopped laughing and signed the contract also.

Mother Bertha Thanked Cindy's parents and informed them that Cindy will begin recording right away. "How much money will she be getting?" stated Mrs. Tucker. "We can sure use some funding around here," she stated. Mother Bertha stated, "well, it depends on how well her Compact Discs (CD's) sells; there is not a lot of money in Gospel music. Cindy just wants to sing because she enjoys singing, thank you both so very much." "Oh, okay," Mrs. Tucker stated. Cindy thanked her parents and walked Mother Bertha home. Cindy faithfully met with the producer, singing, and recording for two years. She continued to visit and care for Mother Bertha; attend school, church services, and doing chores at home. Cindy, now fifteen years of age had recorded four gospel CD's. Although, the CD's were great (in the producer and Mother Bertha's opinion), sells were low. Mother Bertha (now 75 years of age) health was beginning to decline.

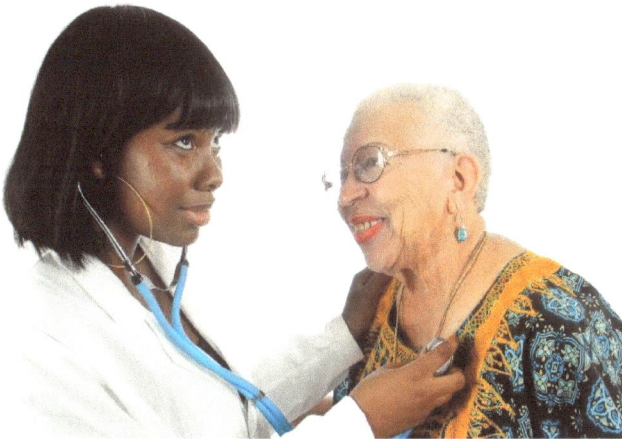

Because of Mother Bertha's failing health, she was in and out of the hospital which brought great sadness to Cindy. Although Mother Bertha informed

Cindy that she was tired of her failing health and wanted to go home to be with the Lord, Cindy continued to pray to God for Mother Bertha to be healed, for this was her only true friend. It was now well over a month that Mother Bertha was admitted in the hospital and Cindy visited her every day. One day Mother Bertha (weak and weary) told Cindy that she believed God was going to call her home soon. Cindy became so distraught; she didn't know what to do or say. Holding back tears, she started singing one of Mother Bertha's favorite songs to her. Mother Bertha just smiled, for she loved Cindy's singing (her voice was soothing) and was so proud of her improvements. Surprisingly staff from various departments of the hospital came rushing to see who was singing so heavenly.

They all clapped after Cindy completed the song, and told her she needed to record her beautiful voice. Cindy informed them that Mother Bertha taught her and that she had already recorded. She gave them the contact information, and many of them stated they would purchase her CD's. Mother Bertha smiled; hugged and told Cindy that she was very proud to be her friend and sister in Christ.   Cindy held Mother Bertha really tight and stated, "I thank God for all you have done for me and I love you so very much!" Tears ran down both of their faces. Mother Bertha told Cindy, "don't worry about me, even when I am gone on home you are going to be just fine, for you know the Lord" and "He will never leave or forsake you, do not be afraid . . ." (Deuteronomy 31:8, NIV). "We will see each other again, when we meet in Heaven. Cindy laid aside Mother Bertha, continued to sing to her until Mother Bertha fell asleep. Before returning home, Cindy stopped by the hospital's chapel and said a prayer for Mother Bertha.

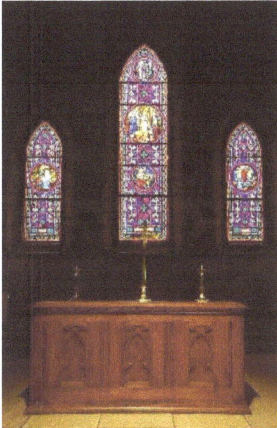

CHAPTER 6
TROUBLE IN THE HOME, PLEASE GOD HELP!

Upon returning home, Cindy found her parents arguing and fighting because Mr. Tucker was fired from his job, her sister Rita was pregnant, and her brother Ralph was arrested and locked up in jail after being with his friends who were selling drugs. The argument started after her parents blamed each other for letting her siblings do whatever they wanted to do. In addition, many bills in the home were now due and Mrs. Tucker's paycheck from working as a teacher's aide was just not enough money to take care of them. Cindy, while thinking about Mother Bertha's condition became overwhelmed until she heard a small voice inwardly saying, pray. Cindy was afraid to ask her parents to pray with her for they always made fun of her and her religion. Nevertheless, she asked them anyway, she stated, "Mom ... Dad..., can we pray together?" They both looked at each other (both drunk) and stated, "what the heck, why not."

Rita, listening in the other room also came out and joined them. Cindy asked them to join hands and bow down on their knees. Shockingly, they did as Cindy suggested. Cindy begins to pray: *"Most High and Faithful God, I come to you as your humble servant along with my family, asking you to forgive us of our sins, strengthen us where we are weak. Please help my family to come to know and depend on you for everything. I know that you can change people, and that you can change any situation in just a twinkling of an eye, if we just have the faith. Dear heavenly Father, help my entire family to recognize that Only you are the King of Kings, and Lord of Lords. Help my family to acknowledge you in all they do. Let them know that you will forgive them of their sins and care for them eternity."*

Cindy prayed on stating, *"Father God . . . strengthen my brother while he is locked up, watch over and protect him. Teach us to love, encourage, and support one another, please instill in us Agape love. Heavenly Father, take care of my dear friend Mother Bertha, thank you for putting her here to lead and guide me to you. You know my heart, in that I do not want her to depart from me, but I know that whatever happens, it is your will and I will respect that. Dear Father, please let Mother Bertha know that I love and appreciate all that she have done for me from the bottom of my heart."*

Cindy begins to cry, but continues to pray. *"Father God, I love my family, and I am angry because all these things has happened to them...if I am not asking too much, please change things for the better . . . if it is your will. In Jesus Name . . . "Talitha Cumi", Amen."* Cindy in completing the prayer noticed that her parents and her sister Rita were crying. They begin to talk peacefully with one another and asked Cindy, what is *Talitha Cumi*? Cindy told them the story about *Talitha Cumi* and they all smiled. Cindy's parents apologized to Cindy for not being there for her or giving her support. Rita apologized to her parents for her situation and to Cindy for always teasing and not supporting or protecting her from other bullies.

Cindy (overjoyed) told them they were all forgiven. Never once had she seen her family come together and talk peacefully with one another. Under her breath she thanked and praised God; she was so grateful and couldn't wait to tell Mother Bertha. While sitting and eating dinner, the telephone rang. Mrs. Tucker answered the phone and came back to the dinner table (her face was saddened) and stated, "Cindy, I am so sorry, that was Mother Bertha's pastor, he called to let you know that Mother Bertha has passed away." Cindy grabbed her mother and started crying, her mother comforted her until she fell asleep. A week later, Cindy's entire family (including Ralph who was out on bail) attended Mother Bertha's Funeral held at her church.

Since Mother Bertha did not have any family, her lawyer Mr. Sam Plenty handled her final requests, will, and funeral arrangements. Over two thousand people attended Mother Bertha's funeral and there were so many beautiful flowers.

Mother Bertha had requested Cindy to sing a solo and play the piano at her funeral. While Cindy's family was happy for her, they were also afraid since the last time they heard her *attempt* to sing she was a little girl, and they couldn't bear it. The song Mother Bertha had requested Cindy to sing was, "The Old Ship of Zion." This Christian hymn was written by M. J. Cartwright around 1889 (Wikipedia, 2016). Mother Bertha loved this song and she felt no one could sing it like her dear daughter in Christ Cindy. Here are the lyrics:

♪ "The Old Ship Of Zion" ♪

Tis the old ship of Zion,
'Tis the old ship of Zion,
'Tis the old ship of Zion,
Get on board, get on board.

It has landed many a thousand,
It has landed many a thousand,
It has landed many a thousand,
Get on board, get on board.

Ain't no danger in the water,
Ain't no danger in the water,
Ain't no danger in the water,
Get on board, get on board.

It was good for my dear mother,
It was good for my dear mother,

It was good for my dear mother,
Get on board, get on board.

It was good for my dear father,
It was good for my dear father,
It was good for my dear father,
Get on board, get on board.

It will take us all to heaven,
It will take us all to heaven,
It will take us all to heaven,
Get on board, get on board.

Cindy set down at the piano, played an intro, and began to sing. Her family was so amazed they didn't know what to do. People who attended the funeral were weeping, wailing, clapping their hands, standing up praising God, and some even ran out of the sanctuary. Yes, Mother Bertha was deeply loved by many. Cindy completed her song and returned to her seat. Her parents grabbed, hugged, and held her very tight. They told her how wonderful she played the piano, sang, and how very surprised and proud they were to be her parents. Her sister and brother were crying and told her she sang beautifully and they loved her.

Cindy, while saddened about the loss of Mother Bertha, was happy her family finally heard her play the piano, sing, and now supported and accepted her. After the crowd settled down, the pastor delivered the eulogy and opened the doors of the church. To Cindy's surprise, her parents, sister, and brother joined the church. Now Cindy was very delighted, gracious, and began to pray inwardly thanking God and Mother Bertha. After the

service ended, many people came to Cindy to thank her
for the wonderful song and told her how beautiful she
sang and played the piano. Cindy informed them that
Mother Bertha taught her. Her parents, sister, and
brother felt very proud to be related to this great young
powerful singer and musician. Cindy, on the other hand
was very heart broken over the loss of Mother Bertha's,
and seeing the casket leave the church and headed for
the cemetery brought copious tears to her eyes.

Cindy and her family returned home and had
dinner together: they kept going on and on about
Cindy's beautiful talents.   From that day forward,
Cindy, her parents, and siblings begin to communicate,
pray, and often attended church together. Still her father
had not found a job and the bills were piling up. Cindy
begins to worry that God did not hear her prayers but,
continued praying and encouraging her family.   Her
brother was awaiting his court date and had no skills to
even look for a job, her sister was unable to work due to
her pregnancy, so Cindy went out to seek work after
school and found a waitress job. She was very happy to

help her family out, but saddened she didn't have time to continue her work in the studio. Cindy soon became tired because she was going to school, working after school, doing her chores at home, and attending church services on Sundays. Often she prayed for God to strengthen and bless her so that she could bless her family.

CHAPTER 7
"TALITHA CUMI" IN PLAIN VIEW

One month after the passing of Mother Bertha, Cindy received a phone call from her producer Mr. Gabriel Wright who was very excited. He told her some good news that almost knocked Cindy off of her feet. The news was that her gospel CD's were selling like hot-cakes to hospitals all around the world. He then informed her that he had a check for her for $1.5 million dollars. Cindy became very nervous and gave the phone to her mother. After her mother heard the check amount, she became nervous and gave the phone to her father, for she thought it was a joke. Mr. Tucker after speaking with Mr. Wright kindly thanked him and stated they would come to the studio. Yes, Mr. Tucker was nervous but, gathered the family and set off to the studio.

Upon arrival, everyone at the studio congratulated Cindy on her new stardom. Cindy and her parents met with Mr. Wright, received the check, thanked him, and left to go directly to the bank, still believing that this wasn't real. The bank supervisor (a past co-worker of Mr. Tucker) Mr. Johnson received the checked and informed them that it was real. The supervisor is now graciously speaking to Mr. Tucker. Cindy's parents, her brother and sister all grabbed her, started cheering, and praising God. What a scene this must have been inside the bank to see this family praising the Lord, other customers in the bank looked on in wonder. Mr. Tucker opened up a bank account for Cindy (also with her parent's name on the account).

Cindy and her family returned home and started paying off the overdue bills. Cindy on the other hand called her job and quit immediately because she was tired and burned-out. She then went to her room, bowed down, and thanked God. Three weeks later, Mother Bertha's lawyer (Mr. Sam Plenty) called to speak to Cindy and her parents to inform them that he needed Cindy and her parents to come to a meeting concerning Mother Bertha's Will. Again, the entire family went along and upon meeting with the lawyer they were informed that Mother Bertha left Cindy her mansion and a trust fund for College (Medical School).

Cindy nearly fainted, and her mother started fanning her. Cindy was very amazed and started crying and thanking God. The entire family gratefully thanked the lawyer. Cindy and her parents signed the needed paperwork and the lawyer gave the deed to Mother Bertha's mansion to Cindy's parents along with paperwork concerning the trust fund. While Cindy, her mother, and sister were still praising God for the blessings, Cindy's father (along with Ralph) asked Mr. Sam Plenty if they could speak to him concerning Ralph's arrest and case. Mr. Plenty said "sure," and asked Mr. Tucker and Ralph to have a seat and tell him what happened leading up to the arrest.

Mr. Plenty after carefully and attentively listening to Ralph stated, "So when the police officers read you your rights, did you understand them?" Ralph states, "What rights?" Mr. Plenty stated, "Your Miranda Rights…you know," *"You have the right to remain silent. Anything you say, can and will be used against you in a court of law. You have the right to an attorney. If you cannot afford an attorney, one will be provided for you. Do you understand the rights I have just read to you? With these rights in mind, do you wish to speak to me?"* (*Miranda Warning.org, 2016*).

Ralph stated, "no one read us any rights, they just arrested us and told us to keep quiet, and that's exactly what we did." Mr. Plenty stated, "Are you sure Ralph?" "Yes, I am very sure Mr. Plenty," Ralph stated. "Well, we will see about this," Mr. Plenty stated. Mr. Tucker asked Mr. Plenty how much it would cost to hire him as his son's lawyer. Mr. Plenty stated, "Mr. Tucker, because Cindy was a dear friend of Mother Bertha, I am going to do this case Pro Bono" (which means free of charge). Mr. Tucker and Ralph bewilderedly (confused) look at each other with tears in their eyes; they hugged, thanked, and shook Mr. Plenty's hand. Upon returning home, Mr. Tucker informed Mrs. Tucker, Cindy, and Rita what had happened at the lawyer's office and the entire family came together and prayed to God in thanksgiving.

Two weeks passed, and now it was court day for Ralph. Mr. Tucker and Ralph entered the courtroom in which Ralph's hearing was held, and as promised Mr. Plenty was present to defend him. The Judge now called for the arresting officers to come forth in regards to Ralph's case, and to *God be the Glory*, the arresting officers was a no show. The Judge now allowed Mr. Plenty to defend his case according to Ralph statements. The Judge looked at Ralph and asks him, "are these statements true" and Ralph stated, "Yes your honor." The Judge stated, "God must be smiling down on you young man, for this is your lucky day. I am going to dismiss this case, and young man, I do not want to see you back in my courtroom again, is that clear?" Ralph stated, "Yes your honor, and thank you so very much!" Mr. Tucker and Ralph were teary eyed, hugged, thanked, and shook Mr. Plenty's hand again, and returned home. The entire family was overjoyed to hear this good news, so they prayed and thanked God for the deliverance.

By the Grace and Mercy of God, the Tuckers' home, situational, and financial crises were now resolved. Cindy was very happy and praised God every day for His blessings, for she now felt the love and togetherness she so longed for from her immediate family and others. Cindy did not forget God, her church, or what Mother Bertha taught her concerning tithing and offerings. Cindy paid tithes from all of her financial substances (work, proceeds from her CD's, and trust fund) to her church. She also donated the mansion (willed from Mother Bertha) to her church to use as a shelter for the poor, for it had 8 bedrooms. Cindy continued to attend church regularly, sing in the choir, and record more Gospel CD's. Her Pastor Rev. Paul Dugood (who always prayed and encouraged her) was very gracious, thankful, and proud to have Cindy and her family as his members.

Cindy now sitting in her bedroom (overjoyed) takes out time to thank God for turning her life and family around for the betterment. She reads her Bible and meditates on His Word for several hours. Her focused is now turned to how things miraculously changed in her life, all because of her faith and belief in God. Cindy credited this all to Mother Bertha, who introduced her to God. She smiles and then sheds tears in remembrance her dear sweet friend; Mother Bertha. "I know my dear friend is in heaven, thank you Heavenly Father for lending her to me for a little while" she stated inwardly.

Cindy (now focused on her singing career) was curious concerning who purchased her CD's that brought in the great revenue. She later learned that God was working behind the scene on her behalf. She found out that not only did, the staff at the hospital purchase her CD's; they spread the information around to their friends in other hospitals. Just like that, Cindy's CD's were purchased by numerous hospitals all over the world for the sole purpose of soothing patients in distress. While attending school with her new stardom, she no longer was teased, but everyone wanted to be her friend. Cindy's Father found a new job at another bank, was promoted as branch supervisor, and joined the male chorus at church.

Cindy was very proud and happy for her father, for *"The glory of children, are their fathers"* (Proverbs 17:6). Cindy's brother Ralph continued going to church and became a junior deacon, *Praise the Lord!*

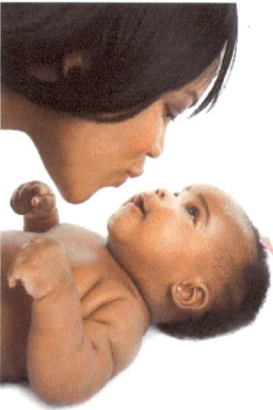

Cindy's sister Rita gave birth to a baby girl whom she named Cynthia, enjoyed and continued to attend church regularly, met a nice young man (at church), and three years later they were married.

Cindy's mother also continued attending church faithfully and invited her friend who joined.

Cindy, upon graduating from High School attended Yale University where she obtained her medical degree at the age of 26. Four years later, Cindy married a young man by the name of Robert Jordan, who she met in medical school; they now have a baby girl in which they named "*Talitha Cumi* Bertha Jordan." Cindy and her family continues to attend church faithfully, for they all love to praise God and greatly appreciates Him for all He has done for their entire family. ***The End!***

Conclusion

Again, the moral of this story is to encourage all readers to come to Christ, love, inspire, encourage, and support our children. In coming to Christ, one must study His Word to learn of Him, lean and depend on Him, and to be empowered by the Holy Spirit God embeds in us. In being empowered by God through Jesus Christ we must learn to use our authority to speak victory over our children and over our dire situations. Our children really need us to be model parents and most of all good examples as God' Stewards. This book is not an attempt for one to try and raise one from the dead as Jesus and some of His disciples did through His power and authority, but in reading this story, one can expect to raise their circumstances from the dead and find hope and comfort during our trials and tribulations by trusting, depending, believing, and calling upon the Name of Jesus for deliverance.

Yes, this story is fictional; however, through Christ one can speak victory over unwanted circumstances, providing it's in His permissive will. Let us come to learn of Jesus, fear God (in Reverence and Respect) and not man. Let us love our children and others. For God hath not given us the spirit of fear; but of power, and of love, and of a sound mind (2ⁿᵈ Timothy 1:7). *Talitha Cumi* in a sense related to this story means boldly trusting, believing, and having unwavering (solid) faith in Christ to change any given situation. *Paraphrased*: For we can do all things through Christ who strengthens us (Philippians 4:13). God grants us power under His authority to speak victory over circumstances, in Jesus' Name.

Our Lord and Savior stated in Matthew 17: 20 .
. . "I say unto you, If ye have faith as a grain of mustard
seed, ye shall say unto this mountain, remove hence to
yonder place; and it shall remove; and nothing shall be
impossible unto you." We as individuals often lose faith
due to our weak carnal minds. Yet in Christ, we are
strengthened and empowered. Even Abraham's wife
had some doubts concerning the power of our Almighty
God. Our Lord questioned Abraham in regards to his
wife Sarah laughing when He informed them they
would bear a child in their old age. *Paraphrasing:* Our
Lord asked Abraham (Genesis 18:14), *if anything was
too hard for God to accomplish?* So what if Abraham
was 100 years old and his wife Sarah was 90 years of
age, yet God can do anything, anytime, anywhere, and
for anyone in His own timeframe. And yes, it came to
pass; Abraham and Sarah gave birth to a son Isaac.

There is nothing impossible for God to handle.
Jesus confirms this in Matthew 19:26 stating . . . "With
God all things are possible." In Jesus' Name let us speak
Talitha Cumi over our children lives, our children
endeavors, spiritual weaknesses, illnesses, situational
crisis, educational endeavors, government issues,
finances, and anything else that needs to be resolved, in
Jesus' Name. God is a good God, He loves us, He wants
to bless us, and give us the desires of our hearts. Most
importantly, God has given us (His servants) power
under His Authority (Luke 10:19). There is *Power in
the Name of Jesus* (Mark 16:17; John 14:13; Acts 4:12,
4:30; Romans 10:13) to break every chain (psalms 107:
14). *Bless you, Talitha Cumi, in Jesus' Name!*

References

Bible Study Tools (2014). *Talitha cumi.* Retrieved from http://www.biblestudytools.com/dictionary/talitha-cumi/

Hudson, J. (June, 2016). Michigan kids organize carwash to help homeless man. *Breitbart.* Retrieved from http://www.breitbart.com/big-government/2016/06/27/michigan-kids-organize-car-wash-to-help-homeless-man/

Kennedy, S. (June, 2012). What motivates kids to help others? *Greater good in action: Science-based practices for a meaningful life.* Retrieved from http://greatergood.berkeley.edu/article/item/what_motivates_kids_to_help_others

Miranda Warning.org (2016). *What are your Miranda rights?* Retrieved from http://www.mirandawarning.org/whatareyourmirandarights.html

Strehler, D. (2016). Truth *for kids: Exciting Bible truths for kids.* Retrieved from http://www.truthforkids.com/age-characteristics/#.Vxak4r3mvDw

Theopedia (n.d.). *Gospel of Mark.* Retrieved from http://www.theopedia.com/gospel-of-mark

The Holy Bible. (2011). New International Version (NIV). *Biblica Incorporation.* Retrieved from https://www.biblegateway.com/passage/?search=Romans%2015:1-7

The Holy Bible. (1998). King James Version (KJV). Large print compact edition. *Holman Bible Publishers:* Korea.

Wikipedia (March, 2016). The old ship of Zion. *Wikipedia, the free encyclopedia.* Retrieved from https://en.wikipedia.org/wiki/The_Old_Ship_of_Zion.

About The Author

Dr. Juanita Crawford background includes: Nursing Professor (Licensed Practical Nurses (LPN) and Registered Nurses (RN), Gospel Soloist, Church Nurse, and Housewife. Her Doctorate Degree is in Education and her Master's Degree is in Nursing. Hobbies includes: Singing, Reading, Writing Books & Poetry, Arts and Crafts, and spending quality time with family and friends.

With GOD *All Things Are*
Possible!